Network Marketing Master Plan

How to Go From Newbie to Network Marketing Rock Star in Less Than a Year

Michael T. Robbins

Published in The USA by:

Success Life Publishing

125 Thomas Burke Dr.

Hillsborough, NC 27278

Copyright © 2015 by Michael T. Robbins

ISBN-10: 1511872047

Disclaimer

Every effort has been made to accurately represent this book and its potential. Results vary with every individual, and your results may or may not be different from those depicted. No promises, guarantees or warranties, whether stated or implied, have been made that you will produce any specific result from this book. Your efforts are individual and unique, and may vary from those shown. Your success depends on your efforts, background and motivation.

Table of Contents

Introduction

You probably have an image in your head of what network marketing, also known as direct sales or multilevel marketing might be. You may have met students, housewives, and people who consider this a part-time job, calling you in for a meeting or orientation and presenting you with their various products—cleaning supplies, vitamins, supplements, financial services, etc.—telling you how easily you could become financially free if you join them.

That is a small part of what network marketing is, but network marketing is still so much more. We know that there may be a huge number of marketing strategies in the realm of business, but this kind of marketing strongly upholds selling of goods and services by word of mouth. It can be the most effective method of sales, especially when the message comes from someone we trust. Network marketing is also a method of marketing that is popular among those who are looking for part-time and flexible hours since this type of business can easily fit different time schedules depending on the sales representative.

Network marketing on a basic level, involves individual agents serving as sellers and distributors of the company's products and at the same time recruiting people to become individual agents as well—that is, creating a network. It is important to note that network marketing is not meant to annoy or bug friends, family members, acquaintances, and strangers, but it is rather a business that is meant to help other people earn money and become successful entrepreneurs.

Throughout this book I will show you how to build a highly successful network marketing business. If you read this book with focus and apply what you learn there will be no limit to your potential!

Chapter 1:

The In's and Out's of Network Marketing

Network marketing or multi-level marketing (MLM) pays sales representatives or distributors commissions not only for the products they sell but also for sales sold by others they recruit. These individuals sell products to the public directly through word of mouth. In addition, a firm utilizing network marketing offers a rewards program to motivate its salespeople to create and manage their own sales teams. Other terms that stand for network marketing include one-to-one marketing, word-of-mouth marketing, face-to-face marketing, gossip marketing, and connected marketing.

History

The history of multi-level marketing can be traced back to 1945 when a company called Nutralite founded by Carl Rehnborg developed network marketing as a means of turning consumers into distributors. Compared to the traditional way of doing business, it is a different way of selling products to the user. In traditional marketing, products made by the manufacturer are sold to retail shops, which in turn sell them to consumers. Network marketing, on the other hand, eradicates the participation of retail shops in the process as products made by the manufacturer end up straight to the consumer. This, among other reasons, is why MLM is a convenient and cheaper business venture since it cuts off some expenses incurred in other types of marketing.

Another way that MLM can cut costs is through the lack of advertisements. Entrepreneurs can utilize various and diverse strategies in order to advertise their products and spread the word about them, some of which include online marketing and traditional dispersal of product knowledge. However, there is one thing that companies may lack but a potential sales representative can provide and that is a network. Each person has an individual network of friends, families, and acquaintances and this network is what companies would like to tap and reach.

Compared to the traditional marketing wherein organizations have to invest millions of dollars every year to inform and entice customers into patronizing their products, the relay of information achieved through networks is much cheaper, faster, and easier. They are aware of how powerful and effective word-of-mouth marketing is because the message comes from those we know and trust.

Advantages

Commercials and TV ads are at times insufficient in persuading customers into buying products. Seeing TV commercials is an impersonal endeavor, an activity that could create a sense of detachment and indifference in the part of the viewer. A customer may feel like the message of the product is not really for them and this leads them to not pay attention to the advertisement. In contrast, customers targeted by network marketing are briefed about and introduced to the product most likely by someone they know. Not only does familiarity breed a trust in the messenger's information and opinion, knowing the person selling you the product is a more intimate process. Customers feel more involved in the transaction.

The benefits you can gain from engaging in and building a multi-level marketing business are numerous and not limited to cheaper running costs. Below are just some of the advantages network marketing has to offer:

The needed capital investment is low.

There is little risk in getting started with an MLM program. Compared to MLM businesses, traditional ones need a large amount of startup cost and the risk of failure will debilitate you from actually starting, because if you don't succeed, you will lose a lot of money.

You do not need to be a network marketer full time. You can participate in other endeavors and do MLM on a part-time basis.

You do not need any experience in terms of marketing in order to set up a business.

There are a lot of products and services that you can center your business around and you are assured of customers patronizing them.

The income potential in network marketing is promising. When you are in traditional businesses, there is a limit to what you can earn despite the perseverance you have put into your work and the hours you have spent building the business. You have a salary bracket set for the position you are in. In an MLM program, you are not restricted by a standard since it is up to you how much you will earn. Your position as a network marketer will not hold you back as long as you have learned the necessary skills and you possess the dedication, perseverance, and stamina among others.

As mentioned, MLM programs require low running or operating costs. Running the business will not rob you of the money you are earning.

Compared to traditional marketing, you are free to move and act. The hours are flexible compared to the traditional office hours wherein you have to be on the job for a fixed number of hours.

Pyramid Schemes

All the aforementioned benefits that you can achieve from building a multi-level marketing business will motivate you towards taking the first steps to being a successful network marketer someday. However, one should be careful in becoming a sales representative for an MLM business since not all multi-level marketing plans are legitimate and legal. Some of them are what you call *pyramid schemes* wherein the money earned is based on the number of people you have recruited and your sales to them rather than on the sales you garner from the consumers who bought your products. This means that in pyramid schemes, products being sold by the manufacturers and bought by consumers are not in the picture. *Money* is, therefore, the product. Compared to distributors in a legitimate network marketing company who make money from the sale of the product, those from pyramid schemes basically just set a financial arrangement wherein people can earn money by the mere recruitment of other people.

With everything said, there will never be a 100% guarantee of success if you limit your skill set and knowledge of network marketing to just the basics. The twenty-first century has seen a boom in MLM programs but not all of them survive. So, why do individuals play in their attempts?

For one, some individuals do not have a concrete goal and objective in mind in starting up their business. They end up getting lost and confused along the way since they do not know to what extent they would take their business. Others start a business on a whim without proper planning and thought. Along the way, it also will be revealed that there is no commitment on the part of the people involved. Other issues sometimes arise from your attitude itself. Giving up when immediate results are not attained, getting discouraged at the slightest setback, and letting lack of self-esteem get in the way. Even your professionalism could affect how well you succeed. If you have set up appointments, you should keep them. You should follow up on your potential prospects. Subsequently, you must always remember to appear professional and organized.

Some also fail because they have not completely grasped what network marketing is and what it is not. Network marketing is not a lot of things. Network marketing is not child's play of talking and gossiping. Mere interpersonal communication from the messenger to the consumer is not what it is all about. It might seem easy but it is a serious business, nonetheless.

Network marketing, is not a get-rich-quick-scheme and it is not a venture based on luck. Success lies on how well you follow basic principles that will guide you on your path. It is not about taking advantage of the people you know – your friends and relatives – even if sharing the information about the product or service to them is the basic foundation of network marketing.

The factors discussed, among others, could prove to be an obstacle in your career as a network marketer. But do not fret. You will succeed provided you are properly equipped with the right knowledge and skills. Some of these elements contributing to most people's failure in network marketing will be addressed in this book.

Chapter 2:

Getting Started the Right Way

Easing Out From another Profession

Network marketing is usually started part-time because of the flexibility of its time schedule in meet-ups, orientations, and selling of goods and services. However, it requires full-time dedication and maximizing your time to really generate income.

As a sales representative, you can determine what time-management session works best for you. Do something to forward your business every day and contact a number of prospects daily. Guide yourself with a weekly plan or set schedules every day of the week with prospects. Keep a daily record of how you utilized your time each day and the number of people you were able to persuade so you can determine your efficiency and effectiveness.

Once you understand the techniques and the process of building a network marketing business, how do you know when it is time for you to ease out of your job and fully engage in network marketing as your full-time job?

First, you need to be sure you have a stable income from network marketing. The pay should be at or higher than the pay of your full-time job. This way, you can be sure that network marketing can sustain your lifestyle and not leave you empty-handed in the end. Have at least three strong leads in your downline, as well. This way, you can be assured that your network will continue to grow and expand, translating to continuous earnings. Lastly, you have to trust your momentum. Once your network marketing business is fast-paced, consistent, and moving forward, your instincts will tell you that network marketing, as a full-time business more than possible.

Taking the Lead: On Building the Downline and Being the Upline

The nature of network marketing is selling goods and services by word-of-mouth. However, the sales force, who are often called distributors, consultants, sales representatives, and individual agents, do not only earn by selling the products and services of the company but also by getting revenues from the sales of agents that they have recruited into the sales force. This is called the "downline". The individuals recruited by one sales representative into the network are his or her "downline". The moment you join network marketing out of an agent or sponsor's recruitment, then that sponsor, is called your "upline".

The exponential growth of your earnings will greatly be affected by the success of your downline. Building a large quantity of quality downlines does not happen easily, building it takes a lot of effort and time from you as a sales representative. In this kind of business, a sales representative does not merely sell products but the job as well.

As an individual agent, start off by recruiting individuals into your downline by finding and contacting people who may be interested in the product or service your business offers. If they aren't really interested in the product or service instead try and sell them on the benefits of network marketing itself. Once you get people to join that are ready to get started building their own downlines, you will find that your sales and earnings can begin to increase at a rapid rate.

As their upline, your job is to train, coach, and develop the skills of your downline for continuous improvement that they may be able to build their own downlines as well.

Chapter 3:

Finding and Keeping the Best Recruits

The members of your downline don't just appear the moment you join, it takes work to get those recruits. Take note that it takes just as much time and effort to recruit a new team member as it does to maintain the downline. Before you build your downline, you have to ask yourself what kind of members you want to be part of your downline—whether you focus on skills, behavior, or attitudinal aspects. Knowing what kind of people you could be working with will save you a lot of time on training, so choose well. Then move on to identifying people who may have the interest and skills to become part of the business and contact these people.

Prospecting merely answers what kind of people you want in your downline, who these people are, where you can find them and when is the best time to contact them. Then you can choose the best way to present to them your goods, services, and process of network marketing and convince them to join your team.

Problems of Network Marketing

Like any other kind of business, network marketing also

involves risks that some people aren't brave enough to face. People in this field of business often encounter problems finding other like-minded individuals to join them.

Problem 1: When your prospect says "Isn't this a scam?"

It can be quite difficult to convince people to join your network if they already have negative preconceptions about what network marketing is all about. It may be the ineffectiveness of the products they once used under another network marketing business or the difficulty of looking for prospects. However, you can change their mindsets by addressing their false ideas about the business.

Solution: Show them that your network is different from what they have experienced in the past. You can always highlight your products and services. Or you can share personal success stories that could inspire your prospects to join you.

Problem 2: When you tell yourself "I am running out of prospects!"

Oftentimes, turned off prospects translate to running out of prospects to call. The next thing you know, your list is as empty as your earnings could be. But do not fret; we have a solution for you.

Solution: There will always be someone out there who is interested in what you are offering. The key is to never stop trying. Unless the prospect firmly tells you, *"No, never contact me again."* Always make a follow up. You may get rejected the first time you meet with your prospects but ask permission if you may call or see them again from time to time just in case they change their mind.

Problem 3: When the people in your downline tell you "We can't stay"

Another problem is keeping your downline productive while they are under your management. Every job or business will always have a turnover rate, and network marketing is no different.

Solution: Your downline may experience difficulties both in selling and recruiting other individuals into the network. For that reason, as their upline, you have to monitor and help your downline when needed. Mentor if necessary and lead them with baby steps one day at a time. If your downline sees your perseverance and support, rest assured you will gain respect for your dedication to the network, and turnover will be kept to a minimum.

Finding the Best Prospects and Persuading Them

In order to have a successful and productive downline, you must first bring the right people into the network. The question, though, is how? Here are the steps:

Make a list. Making a list is key to having the best prospects for your downline. All you have to do is keep a never-ending list of people to contact.

Make another list. This list must contain more than just random names of people you simply know. This list should be for people who you know for a fact are interested in the product or service your company offers. These people will be more willing to join your team since they are already interested in what they would be offering as a team member. These people should also be the types who are independent and motivated such as yourself. They will have a burning desire to succeed and more than likely will be interested in the opportunity you are offering. This would save you the time of sitting through uncomfortable and awkward conversations and continuously taking rejections.

People who already have experience in entrepreneurship or handling their own businesses would be great prospects for network marketing. They know how business works, and more than likely they know how to sell themselves. You could also target sales professionals such as realtors, sales agents, and accountants. They usually have people skills that can make it easy for them to grow a network marketing business. Having these kinds of people in your downline could save you time and stress, as they will be more prepared to not only grow the downline, but also train their own team members as the network grows.

Although, experience may not always be an indicator of success, it will save you time and effort. It creates a downline that can be much more effective and efficient.

Call them. You should now start calling or contacting your list of prospects. Ask them if they would be interested in hearing about a wonderful new opportunity. An opportunity to build a profitable business and at the same time helping others to build a substantial residual income as well.

Meet-up with them. After a prospect has agreed to meet with you schedule an appointment to present the opportunity. Meeting over lunch or dinner is a great idea as is meeting at their location. Whatever kind of meeting you prefer, always prepare your presentation before hand. Think of any possible questions your prospect could ask and be prepared to answer these questions. Never go unprepared, as this will kill your chances of landing the prospect. Remember this orientation is your first and most likely last chance of persuading your prospect so do not waste this meeting.

Win them. If you get rejected at the meeting, don't fret! You can still ask for permission to follow up with them later. However, if you win them the first time, you will have more time to win other prospects as well. So you have to begin orientations building from your prospects' interests. Do not dive immediately into the business. Build and build. Begin by establishing a warm welcome and greeting, letting your prospect become comfortable with you. Then you can open up with all the benefits he or she could get by joining you. Listen to what these prospects might want to know. What they tell you may be the key to how you could persuade them. They might tell you what they want, what their goals are, or what their current status in life is – anything. This will allow you to tailor your proposal to fit their needs and up your chances of getting a 'yes!'

Chapter 4:

Recruiting and Training Your Downline

Recruiting

Your business would be pointless without the people in your downline because network marketing is really a business that needs the power of others. To start bringing people into the network, make the most of your time with a targeted list or a "warm list." That is, make a list of all the people you know or are acquainted with from high school to college, work, church, gym, or wherever and plan who to call. Even go so far as to make a schedule to hold yourself accountable for whom you will call and when. Starting with those you know may be interested makes it much less intimidating. Call at least 2 of your prospects every day. By the end of a quarter, you have called almost 200 people! Imagine the number of "Yes's" you could get from that number. By the end of a month or two, you most definitely already have people in your downline—maybe even after the first week.

But how do you actually sit there and talk about your business?

The key is to be friendly, yet firm. You can always begin by

introducing yourself, of course. In the shoes of your prospect, imagine how awkward it would be if you both sat there, discussing and talking about business and realizing, in the end, that you do not have any idea who you are actually talking to. So, keep it simple. Although you may have introduced yourself over the phone, introducing yourself personally will still feel warmer.

After you've gone over introductions, you can proceed with presenting the mechanics of network marketing and also how their earnings have the potential to grow exponentially. Share success stories from your own personal business to show these potential team members just how promising and successful a network marketing business can be. However, keep in mind that it is more important to win your prospects by integrity and not exaggeration.

Still, despite all your efforts, your acquaintances, friends, and even relatives could reject your offer. But do not be disheartened; remember that they are rejecting the opportunity you are offering. It isn't anything personal against you, your friendship or the relationship that you have with this person. So simply thank them for their time and move on. The rejection does not have to change anything. You can ask your prospects who gave a "No" if they have a couple of friends who may be interested in the business. Doing things this way keeps it more personal and also means you probably won't run out of any potential contacts anytime soon. So you see, there is a way to turn a "No" into another probable "Yes."

The key, all throughout the recruitment process, is to never give up. Continue making conversations about your company's products and services to new people every single day. Be sure to always carry a brochure, business card, or even a sample product with you at all times. This could serve as a prompter for conversations at convenient times and places with people who might be interested and that way you never miss a good business opportunity, simply by being prepared and planning ahead. You can also advertise online through social networks or blogs, or even ad spaces on related business sites to attract more people into your line and to give people a chance to contact you as well.

Training

Being a sales representative requires you to be dynamic, enthusiastic, and well versed. The position has high competition in the market, so your network marketing skills need to be well polished and set you apart.

When training your sales representatives, begin by showing them *what's in it for them*. Show them how the network marketing techniques you are presenting to them will increase their sales percentages and how this increase translates to bigger earnings. Keep your training presentation interesting and interactive—the more hands on the better.

Remember, you are training them to become more productive and hardworking team members. The more you keep the spark of interest in them alive, the more they will want to listen to what you have to share, and the more they can learn. You can do this by providing and sharing real situations, stories and examples of how certain techniques in selling and recruiting new members of the downline worked for you.

Another effective strategy is to have them role-play with each other and you as if they were speaking to potential prospects. This way you have a chance to show them proper sales techniques and correct anything that they don't understand before they ever meet with a real prospect.

You can also encourage sharing of experiences from those who have some sales experience and the techniques that have worked for them in the past. Knowing what really works in the market and real-life situations of selling and recruiting will definitely help your downline in working their way into convincing their customers and/or prospects.

Do not end with a single training session, though. New techniques need to be developed from time to time and can benefit your entire downline. So, share and conduct training sessions from time to time, especially when you feel there are issues that need to be addressed.

Remember that network marketing is a business that highly demands competitiveness among sales representatives and it is your responsibility to share what you know to your downline so you all keep up with the changes in the business.

Dealing with Rejection

Heartbreaks are possible in business. There is the potential of rejection from a prospect and their "No" might sting. However, you shouldn't dwell on this or take it personally.

In network marketing, each person you are introduced to will have different viewpoints, needs and desires. They will have different goals for their life that may not necessarily fit into what you're offering. That's just how it goes.

However, there are things you can do to ensure that you keep growing your downline. The main thing is to stay positive and focus on a variety of different prospects. The more prospects you meet with, the more chances you have of getting a "Yes." This goes with keeping a never-ending list of prospects and scheduling meetings with them to hold them accountable.

Once you have set appointments with your prospects this should give you some hope. Only those that are interested, no matter how slightly, will show up. If you can get them to come to your meeting you are that much closer to reeling them in. Never waste a business meeting—it is sometimes your only shot at securing this person and getting them to say "Yes," so once you've got them, be sure to keep their attention.

The only thing you have to do now is to build from that interest no matter how big or small it might be. You can start by building up rapport between you and your prospects. Be friendly but firm, not just by what you say but also by your gestures. Impressions may change in time but in first meetings, they play a huge role. Once you have established rapport and a friendly air between you and your prospect, it will be easier to ease your business in.

Next, start presenting the wide array of products and services your company can offer to them and their possible prospects. Show them all the benefits they can gain from being a part of what you have to offer. Stress that in network marketing, the more people you have on your side the faster and easier it is to multiply and leverage your income.

After, or even while you are presenting, your prospects may have questions regarding the products or services or the process of network marketing. All you have to do is listen. The fact that your prospects have questions shows that they are interested. Address their questions and concerns with positivity and honesty.

However, sometimes no matter how persuasive you may be, a prospect is just going to say, "No." Take it in stride.

In all cases of rejection, these prospects are not rejecting you; they are rejecting the opportunity that you are offering them. So don't take it personally. It may be because of time constraints. It may be because of personal matters and problems that hold them to their decision of saying "No" to your offer. You cannot always win over everyone.

Qualified leads and people will not reject you because they have the same disposition and spark in network marketing as you do. And if you have leads like this in your line, the more productive your line will and can be.

Always continue widening your network by evaluating your approaches in recruiting, too. Think about and assess your ways of recruiting by examining what led to what—a rejection or a success. Sharpen your strengths and work on your weaknesses. If you are experiencing self-doubt, you can always call someone from your upline. He or she brought you in because they knew you were capable and had the desire to succeed in this kind of business. So reach out and get help when you need to.

Chapter 5:

Building Your Business

Meeting your Destined Sales Force

Conducting meetings is a very important activity in the network marketing business. Each individual member of your team needs to feel a sense of belonging. Meetings are a key way to keep those in your downline on board and also emphasizes the fact that they are not doing this business all on their own— they are a part of something bigger, a part of a community that will help them along the way.

Meetings play a key role in the operation of a successful business. One benefit is that it can be an avenue for you to communicate with your target audience. They are also useful for training your downline, announcing vital news and revealing important updates regarding the business.

For network marketing, the fundamental principle of duplication is a rule that will guide you in conducting a successful meeting. First of all, what you need to take note of is the best place to hold your meeting. This is where duplication comes in. You have to choose a place that is easily duplicable. A presentation that cannot be reproduced would be detrimental. Conducting your meetings in a hotel is not advisable because they will not be easily duplicated due to various reasons; the most obvious is that they are expensive. You cannot always hold a meeting in a hotel and this goes against the principle of duplication.

Therefore, when you take into account expenses, duplication and comfort—in-home meetings and presentations are most advisable. A home meeting is ideally composed of 4-8 or 10 prospects and commonly held in a living or family room and should always be done in your own home. This way, you have control and power of the situation. Holding sessions on your own turf increases your level of confidence, comfort, and enthusiasm and the other aforementioned factors help you stay in control of the meeting.

Now, when you start your meeting, do not be discouraged if someone does not show up. On average, about half of the people you invite probably won't come. Next time you set a date for a meeting, make sure that there are no special circumstances (e.g. holidays) that would lead to your meeting being an inconvenience. To add, do not complain about the attendance during the meeting. Do not comment on how many people are not present. Focus instead on the people who came and pay attention to them.

Another important point to remember is if you are the owner of the house you are holding your meeting at, you need to be the one who opens and closes the meeting. Even if another person is there who has a higher position than you, say an upline, who is responsible for doing the presentation, the homeowner must be the one to welcome and gather guests.

When doing your introduction, do not start off strong as it may turn your prospects off. Remember to be professional and at the same time, open and friendly. Your closing remarks, on the other hand, should be strong and exacting. Show your prospects that this business is serious and will reap results in order to encourage them to sign-up.

During the meeting, avoid using industry jargon in your presentation because those who are not yet part of the business (your prospects) will not understand. You will either then have to spend extra time explaining those terms or risk losing their interest all together. The worst case is that you use unfamiliar terminology, unaware that your prospects didn't understand and your prospects don't ask for clarification. At the end of the day, they will be leaving your meeting confused.

After the meeting, ensure that you have some time to talk to the people who came and seek out feedback. In cases where you hear a negative response from someone, don't let the disappointment or any other feeling stop you from being a professional. Accept their remarks and recognize their thoughts. Don't be involved in a public clash of dissenting opinions.

You also need to follow up with the people who attended your meeting. It is a must for you to take note of every guest and their contact details so you can follow up with them. A sign in book works well for this. Afterward, inquire about their attitude towards the presentation and from there, depending on the cues that your prospects exhibit, proceed with recruiting them further into the business or letting them go.

Enthusiasm is not just for Cheerleaders

Network marketing, no matter how numerous its benefits, is still subject to the usual problems that businesses in general face. Attrition, resistance, and other forms of discouragement will lie in your way and will demotivate you from pushing towards the success you are aiming for. What you need to always remember is to rise up against these challenges and keep pushing forward.

Your personality and the kind of attitude you embrace will greatly steer your career. Network marketing requires you to be the type of individual who is continually enthusiastic about what he or she is doing. This positive attitude will attract other individuals.

In times of great disenchantment and dissatisfaction with your business, it will not be easy to shake off these undesirable feelings that come along with discontent. But bear in mind that your emotional state and vulnerability to hurdles will affect the way you run your business, your interaction with other people, and your relationships with those around you. Therefore, it is necessary to get rid of negative emotions in order to function at your best and inspire others to be a part of your team. Negativity will not create an ideal working environment and it will just pull other people down. There area number of ways to maintain your enthusiasm and dispel any ill feelings.

It is advisable to surround yourself with things and individuals that will uphold the spirits in your organization. Working with people who are indifferent, detached, and impartial to your objectives will just curb your enthusiasm with what you are doing.

If you lose a prospect, do not dwell on it and get depressed. It is a fact that attrition is present no matter what industry you are in. If you stay positive and keep building your skills the right people will join your business and you will have a competent arsenal of uplines and downlines by your side.

Channel your negative feelings and emotions into something productive and beneficial to your business. If you call a meeting and there are those who don't show up or end up being uncooperative, do not waste your time on mulling it over and getting stressed. Rumination will not help improve your disposition.

Instead, learn to utilize the energy inside you into activities pertinent to your business. Finding new prospects, organizing the structure of your business, keeping track of your people, among others, are fruitful concerns that you can occupy yourself with.

In short, focus on the present – on the things you need to do and the transactions you need to run a successful MLM business. Keep your eyes on the business goals you want to fulfill. "The past is past" is a cliché that is necessary to remind us not to dwell on our mistakes and shortcomings.

Furthermore, you can also engage in activities that would normally lift your spirits up. In addition, cultivating inspiring, enriching, and positive thoughts will also help. If the source of your problems and irritation is a person, you would do well to avoid him or her temporarily in order to collect yourself. If you cannot do that, entertain them as quickly and as well as you can in order to get past the issue of interacting with them.

Focus is not Hocus Pocus

Networking marketing is a competitive business and getting lost in the bustle could be your demise. One of the reasons why some people fail in network marketing is that they lose sight of the goals they wanted to achieve. Focusing on the end goal and even on the moment-to-moment happenings goes a long way to helping you survive the unstable waters of the fast-paced and dynamic world of business.

Organization is key to a successful industry. It reduces the risk of chaos that would lead you to being distracted from key actions that you have to execute. While some people thrive in disorder, organizing your time, activities, and plans makes for a more efficient and effective operation. You can make use of different methods in order to keep track of the things you have to do or take note of. Make use of technology (e.g. electronic trackers, planners) and even of traditional organizers.

Duplication, one of the fundamental principles of MLM, is not only applied to conducting meetings and prospecting. Keep this principle in mind if you want a centered and focused business. Duplicating systems – meaning, sticking to a system that has been tried and tested– will push you towards success.

Along the way, there will be many events or situations that could cause you to stray from your vision and plan of action. Some of your distributors might leave the company but do not let this make you think that you have to immediately modify the system you are following or that changes must immediately be put into place. Again, it should be reiterated that attrition is a given fact in any industry. Have faith in your system and in your plans of action.

Avoiding the False Genies

You started building an MLM company because you heard of other peoples' stories about their success with it. But perhaps you did so because you were enticed by how network marketing was packaged as a very easy business wherein you can reap the benefits in no time at all. Do not be misled by expectations that are not 100% accurate. Just like with any business, MLM is not as easy as 1, 2, and 3. The bottom line is, you still need to expend effort, hard work, perseverance, strength, dedication and stamina, among other traits for it to work. Moreover, it is not about luck.

There are a lot of facts about network marketing. For one, the income potential that you can gain from an MLM program is huge. It can compete and even win against the salaries of office workers. But again, remember that without work, the promise of a six-figure income will never be fulfilled.

One of the perks of being in the MLM industry is the flexibility of the working hours. You can do it as a part-time job, but do not expect to have the same results as a person who is in MLM full-time.

Attrition is given in the MLM industry; putting false truths and expectations into your distributors' heads only increases that rate. Keep to the truth as close as possible. There is no danger in presenting the highest possibilities of the business to your prospects but make sure that those possibilities are within their reach. If your people find out that they are not achievable or couldn't be achieved in the first place, they will leave the company and tell others about their negative experience. Word of mouth strategy is one of the foundations of this business. You do not want the people who quit your company to go around telling others that you are not credible.

Ensuring commitment

Any dream that we want to come into fruition requires commitment. Commitment guarantees that we do every step towards success with heartfelt determination and passion. Psychological studies have shown that the more committed a person is to what he is doing or to the organization he is in, the less likely that he will quit. How do you ensure the commitment of the people working with you? The answer lies in making them feel involved and invested in your business. If someone is emotionally, physically, and psychologically invested in his or her work, they are more committed to the success of every project.

Another means to ensure commitment is clarifying the vision and mission of your business. If your people are not cognizant of what they are committing themselves to, you will end up with an unreliable and unhappy team.

Conclusion

The network marketing industry has seen an increase in workforce as individuals become aware of the advantages that network marketing has over traditional business models. Numerous companies around the world use network marketing as a strategy because of its effectiveness and efficiency. With that said, you might be encouraged to start your own MLM business, but remember that your path towards success does not just stop with building the business. Knowing the in's and out's of what makes network marketing unique, and applying the right principles and attitude go a long way towards surviving in this fast-paced, dynamic world.

Moreover, just as important as knowing the fundamental aspects of network marketing, putting your heart into the business will help you succeed. Character, attitude, and behavior will determine your stay in the industry especially since MLM requires you to deal with other people. To build a network and form connections it takes a special kind of person, someone with the right perspective and disposition. You are obviously one of these people, or you wouldn't have picked this book up, and read it this far.

With everything that you have learned in this book, you should have the confidence to get out there and build your network. Only when you take the first steps towards success will you begin to achieve success. Congratulations on taking that first step!

Thank you for reading this book and I wish you good luck on your journey and remember to stay focused!

Printed in Germany
by Amazon Distribution
GmbH, Leipzig